D1632419

An Evening with the Book Society

Maria Vassilopoulos has worked in bookselling and publishing for twenty years and is currently Global Sales Manager at University of Wales Press. She recently completed her PhD on the British book trade at University College London. She has also worked with the *Bookseller*, the Society of Young Publishers, and the Bookselling Research Network on various projects designed to preserve and tell the story behind the book trade's history. She is building her own archive of book trade documents.

An Evening with the Book Society

A CELEBRATION OF
100 YEARS OF DINNERS,
DISCUSSION
AND FRIENDSHIP

Maria Vassilopoulos

Marble Hill
London

First published in 2022 by Marble Hill Publishers
Flat 58 Macready House
75 Crawford Street
London W1H 5LP

www.marblehillpublishers.co.uk

ISBN: 978–1–8383036–8–6

Typeset in 11/14pt Monotype Imprint by Barneby Ltd

Jacket design by Linnet Mattey
Text design by Nicky Barneby

Contents

Foreword by
Michael Bhaskar
page vii

Acknowledgements
page ix

Introduction
page 1

1

Walpole's
Little
Dining
Club
page 3

2

The
Committee,
Members
and
Meetings
page 7

3

The
Constitution
and the
Rules
page 15

4

Dinners,
Guests
and
Speakers
page 25

5

The
Speakers
page 31

6

A
Note
on
Authors
page 39

7

Special
Events
page 41

8

The
Afterparty
page 45

9

List of
Presidents
and
Chairs
of the
Book
Society
page 79

Foreword

The Book Society is unique.

It spans publishers, literary agents, printers, book-sellers, wholesalers, scouts, recruiters, industry bodies and sundry other parts of the trade too numerous to mention. This is what makes both the book industry and the Society so wonderful – its range and intricate complexity. So often that is lost in the course of day-to-day business, everyone digging deep into their silo: academic, or sales, or rights, or whatever area it might be. The Society is one of the only places that brings it all together and not only makes sense of this bewildering complexity, but actively celebrates it. It's a wonderful forum, a meeting house, for those engaged in widely dis-parate portions of the industry yet who remain united by a common purpose in which we passionately believe: books, and getting them into the hands of readers. Every-one at the Society has devoted their lives and careers to this mission, and the Society is a testament to it.

The book industry is not only complex, it is, compared to so much of the economy, old. The Society has been going strong for over a hundred years, and its roots go much deeper than that. But like the industry as a whole, this is both a strength – showing the great resilience and long-term outlook of what we do – and also a sign that the Society, like the rest of the industry, is good at adapting, keeping what is most valuable but being nimble at moving with the shifting terrain. The core ingredients stay the same: food, drink, discussion, friendship, laughter, experience, but much changes nonetheless.

That highlights another essential facet of both the book world and the Book Society. They are both built on people, on relationships. This is an industry that thrives on real and meaningful connections, often lasting for many decades. The great edifice of books is built on a million conversations, and the Book Society is one of the biggest, most sprawling and longest lasting of them all. In an era of remote meetings and social media, the value of being in the same room has never been greater.

Entering its second century, the Book Society stands at a similar point to the industry it does so much to embody. Facing challenges, yes, required to look at itself and ensure that it is fit for the future; but also marked with a certain confidence that the storms can be weathered, that the great mission goes on, and the conversation will continue with more vibrancy, excitement and vision than ever.

I, for one, look forward to it.

Michael Bhaskar
The Book Society Chair 2019–2022

Acknowledgements

Thank you to the Book Society for allowing me to tell your story and inviting me to the occasional dinner.

Thank you to Emma Lowe who recommended me to write this history, David Taylor who agreed to the project initially and has stood by it until publication, and to Sue Whitley for the cups of tea and conversation that started me off in my endeavours.

Special thanks to Francis Bennett, who has accompanied me on the full journey and without whom I could not have written this book.

Maria Vassilopoulos

The author and the publishers would like to express their warm thanks to the Book Society and its Committee, to Michael Bhaskar, former Chair of the Society, David Taylor and Nick Singh of Ingram Content Group, Linnet Mattey (for the cover design), Nicky Barneby (for the text design), Jamie Hodder-Williams, current Chair of the Society, Richard Charkin, past President and Amanda Ridout, current President. All set-up, production and distribution costs to members have been donated by Ingram Content Group. Without their help, support and enthusiasm this celebration of the Book Society would not have come into being.

Introduction

The Book Society turned 100 in 2021, and to mark this impressive milestone, I was asked if I would write a short history. I have worked in the book trade all eighteen years of my career, but in 2015 I embarked on studying it and am currently completing a PhD at UCL. Therefore, this project was of great interest to me, and I hope you enjoy the results of my research into the Society and its activities over the last ten decades. I decided that it would be best to base this book directly on the Society's archives, which I accessed through Sue Whitley (a previous Hon. Secretary of the Society) back in 2016. As with much source material of this nature, the minutes, books and copies of letters were stored up until the 2010s, when the archive was made obsolete with the advent of email. Instead of trying to access an indefinite amount of correspondence to try and fit the more recent events, the end of the book will feature comments from those members who were kind enough to answer a few questions about how they view the Society as it is now and what they hope will happen in its next 100 years. The other sections of the book will share some of the past decisions and deliberations of the elected committee and members over the decades, and look at the dinners themselves – not forgetting the staggering number of speakers that have graced them.

The layout of the chapters has been designed to lead you, the reader, through a whole night with the Book Society so that you can take in all these events in the places where they occurred. We will start with the committee meeting, and discover the debates and decisions that have been made from the very beginning of the Society until the resolution that a website was necessary. Then we will head over to the main event, the dinner, which will be held at a surprising number of venues, including, of course, the Savile Club. The speakers of various decades will take to the podium as the plates are cleared away, and the Chatham House Rule will be very much in play, as will the wine. Finally, we will find ourselves clapping the speakers off their stage and continue our conversations with fellow members and their guests. Here's hoping that a night in the Book Society archives will live up to your expectations, and you will see it as a fitting commemoration. However, before we arrive at the committee meeting, I wanted to take you back to the 1920s to tell the story of how the Society began.

1

Walpole's Little Dining Club

The organisation known today as the Book Society[1] began when Hugh Walpole invited British book industry members to dine at his home in York Terrace, London. His biographer, Rupert Hart-Davis, tells of how the prolific novelist called the gathering his 'little dining club' after he suggested a trade dinner in 1920 for that very kind of event to become more regular. Walpole was an extremely successful author after his 1909 bestselling book, *The Wooden Horse*, received critical acclaim in Britain and America, and Hart-Davis – later a chairman of the Society himself, from 1953–6 – described Walpole as warm, gregarious and friendly, so it is not surprising that Walpole had the idea of getting

---

1. NB The Society of Bookmen/the Book Society will also be referred to as 'the Society' throughout.

like-minded industry folk together. If you had found yourself at one of these early meetings in Walpole's drawing room, then you would have seen an impressive pencil portrait of famed explorer Walter Scott framed and hung over the grand fireplace, whilst you waited to be shown to dinner in the spacious dining room. as well as a rarefully working pianola.[2] After the arrival of all his guests, dinner would be served, and the conversation and port would flow once the dishes had been cleared away. As the months went on, the name of the club would be formalised to 'the Last Tuesdays' for a year or so, until the group got larger and there was a will to transform from a dinner club to an actual society.

On 20 October 1921, 26 bookmen, including Walpole in the chair, met at the offices of William Heinemann at 20–21 Bedford Street, London, to settle on an official name; they then appointed the first committee to discuss some formal aims and membership criteria. Those in attendance included G. A. E. Marshall of W H Smith, Sidney Pawling (Heinemann), John Galsworthy (novelist), Frank Denny and J. G. Wilson (booksellers), Harold Macmillan, John Irvine (playwright), Stanley Unwin, Frank Swinnerton (novelist), David Roy (bookseller) and Grant Richards (publisher). However, it was not enough to keep meeting and talking. To co-exist with the Booksellers Association, the Publishers Association and other book trade bodies, the Society needed to decide on a common rationale for their existence. The

---

2. Rupert Hart-Davis, *Hugh Walpole* (London: Sutton Publishing, 1997), pp. 197202–4.-202.

Society's original aims were written out on paper by the committee as follows:

To promote and extend the distribution of books by the co-operation of the various branches in the book trade and to promote opportunities for improving the educational and technical qualifications of those engaged in the distribution of books, with the object of rendering good service to the community, and to co-operate for mutual benefit with other organisations concerned with the creation, production and distribution of books.

Once matters had become more formalised and announced to the wider book industry, the Society began in earnest to fulfil these aims. One vehicle for doing so was the committee meeting. As explained in the introduction to this book, the Book Society's archives were established in the 1920s to record the initial members' actions as the framework was created and rules began to be set for members and guests alike. Although the committee was made up of many different members over the years, the topics they discussed were similar to the concerns of any society, then and now: membership, subscription fees, procuring speakers ... there was the odd scuffle, too, and through ten decades of publishing concerns and challenges, other bigger issues also arose, such as being online, representing the industry's interests, not stepping on the toes of other trade associations, and the modernisation of particular views. The evidence left of these meetings has helped document the evolution of the Society as a living, breathing place of discussion and dissemination of ideas.

2

The Committee, Members and Meetings

When setting up an association or society, apart from settling on a common set of aims, several other practical elements need to be organised. What to charge members and how to collect subscriptions, the setting up of a bank account, discussions over where to hold meetings and then more conversation and debate over who should be invited to join or speak. In the 1920s, the first committee members set about ticking these tasks off their list, starting with choosing a name. On a dull afternoon in November 1921, they met for the first time with Hugh Walpole in the chair at Ye Olde Cock Tavern on Fleet Street, London, to decide what the Society should officially be called. It is recorded in the meeting minutes that there was one suggestion of 'the Octavos', and this came a close second to the favourite, 'the Society of Bookmen', suggested by Marshall. At this point, all the committee were men, so it is no surprise that this was the name they chose, although it would prove a point of discussion and debate as times modernised around the Society at the end of the century. Once a name had been chosen, the rules and constitution started to be discussed, a secretary was eventually employed for £500 a year in 1922, and the search for a permanent home for the meetings began.

However, it was during these very early days of assuming an order over the running of the Society that Walpole decided he wanted to bow out of being Chair. At a committee meeting in January 1922, just a few months after the inauguration, he stated that he was off travelling for at least two years and so felt that he should resign his position. The unanimous response from the committee was to find a way that he could remain involved, and so the role of President was created, and Maxwell was asked to be deputy. Walpole was quite reluctant to accept, but he was persuaded to stay in post until September. However, in early July, a committee meeting took place at Stanley Unwin's office at 40 Museum Street, Bloomsbury, London, and a ballot was held to replace Walpole and Maxwell, who had also resigned his post. Both men had stated that they would be unable to keep to meeting dates due to travel commitments, and the Society decided that going forward, any member who failed to attend several meetings in a row would be asked to leave. This was written into the rules from that September, when Marshall was appointed as the new President. Walpole went on to become chair of a new Book of the Month subscription club called the Book Society, set up by Arnold Bennett in 1929.[3] He also remained the president of his dining club until his death in 1941.

Once the Society was up and running and the committee had been organised, there were matters that needed to be considered by the wider membership. Although there were initial concerns throughout the late 1920s that the Society was treading on the toes of the more established trade associations, the Society was ambitious and soon they were all sharing ideas, such as consulting on a general reduction in the prices of books, the creation of a central book room where public librarians could view new publications, co-operative publicity efforts and seasonal exhibitions for journalists and booksellers. Several lectures were held by members who suggested topics to the committee in the 1920s and 30s, and these were also distributed as circulars or pamphlets. One of the earliest, 'The Classification of Literature' by Frank Pacy, was published in 1922, in which he called for a universal way of categorising books to make them easier to sell, something that did not exist at the time. Then 'The New Reading Public' by Sidney Dark in the same year discussed how publishers should not forget the reader and what they desired to read. In the 1930s, 'Trade or Profession' by Harold Raymond spoke about how simplification of the industry would

---

3. Rupert Hart-Davis, *Hugh Walpole* (London: Sutton Publishing, 1997), p. 299.

aid its growth. Basil Blackwell, in 'The Idea of a British Book Trade Association', suggested that there be one conjoined industry body and then in 'A New Order in the Book Trade', published in 1937 with fears of another war fast approaching, he wrote:

We know that to publishers this violent prosperity of Wartime is likely to bring more harm than good. If we are to believe Stanley Unwin (and who shall dare to disbelieve that formidable man?), publishers are in a sense selling their capital. I am at this moment more concerned about the future of publishing than of bookselling.

Even whilst World War II was raging, the Society was thinking. In March 1943, the renowned publisher Alan Bott wrote 'The Book Trade a Plan for Expansion', where he acknowledged Basil Blackwell's speech as a basis for his idea.[4] All of these circulars are a snapshot of the topics that those in the Society felt needed to be discussed at length by the whole industry.

Amongst the backdrop of these significant ideas and contributions, a long-lasting achievement would come from the minds of publishers Grant Richards and Stanley Unwin. In April 1922, they suggested that there should be a co-operative book society. At a committee meeting, Richards said, in a similar vein to Sidney Dark's 'The New Reading Public', that many people in England would never buy a book and that the book trade should spend more money on advertising because,

---

4. 'The Book Trade a Plan for Expansion', p. 3.

in his view, they did not know the reading public well enough. The Society went on to produce a pamphlet, 'Why Not Books?', which illustrated how the book trade could help enthuse the public about books and publishing in Britain. Included were designs suggested for display materials, and a rationale for the campaign, which began:

It is generally admitted that in the practical appreciation of 'things of the mind' – of which literature is the most extensive and one of the most important – Great Britain lags behind some of the other great national communities of to-day. In France, Germany and probably the United States there exists indisputably a greater readiness to study literature, to read books and to buy them than in this country.

Unwin, who would become President of the Society in 1947, had also put forward that a book trade marketing and publicity co-operative would be a good idea. Throughout his career, he was outspoken about the state of the publishing industry, and he published what were seen by some in the industry as controversial books by the likes of Bertrand Russell, Marx and Freud. Not everyone in the industry accepted him and so Unwin saw the Society as a place he could suggest ideas. The National Book League was formed on 11 September 1924[5] as a subsidiary of the Society, which supported

5. Ian Norrie, *Sixty Precarious Years: A Short History of the National Book League 1925–1985* (London: National Book League, 1985) p. 16.

its establishment with a gift of £100, and committee members including Unwin and also Frank Denny and another publisher Edward Marston were delegated to work there. By November of the same year, Denny had resigned from the Society to focus his attention entirely on the League, and financial ties between the organisations were fully severed in September 1925, although the Society continued to donate to the League for years afterwards. After evolving transitioning through several incarnations, the League now operates as the charity BookTrust.

In the late 1920s, another innovative idea involving a national book token scheme was suggested by Harold Raymond at a meeting of the Society, and all being in favour and thinking it was a wonderful idea, it was duly handed to the League to take forward with the Booksellers Association. In addition, in the late 1930s, the Society committee had the idea of using the medium of television to educate a wider audience about the workings of the British book trade and from this, those at the League went on to create two television documentaries, *Cover to Cover* and *Chapter and Verse*.[6]

After this point, the Society began to concentrate on being a place for conversation rather than implementation but there were still a few other occasions where the committee became involved in pushing through bigger industry change. One of the more notable of these occurred on 1 November 1984. The *Evening Standard*

---

6. Iain Stevenson, *Book Makers: British Publishing in the Twentieth Century* (London: The British Library, 2008), p. 88.

published an article, 'Hands off our Books!', in which the then Society secretary Sally Whitaker warned that 'sparks may fly' over a proposed application of VAT on books by the British government.[7] The article explained that gatherings of the Society were usually a sedate affair, but in this case, 130 people were expected to attend a meeting to discuss what the implications would be for the industry if the government were to get their way. To accommodate the larger attendance that was expected at this particular gathering, the Society moved the venue to the Connaught Rooms in central London. Alex Macmillan, chair of the so-called 'Anti-VAT' working party, spoke to the members and their guests, including author Roy Jenkins and publishing names such as Andre Deutsch, Charles Pick and Olivia Gollancz. The end decision was to zero VAT, and that still stands to this day, although many of you reading this will no doubt be aware that it is still a matter that rears its head on occasion, and could potentially need another such meeting in the future.

---

7. *Evening Standard*, 1 November 1984, p. 45.

3

The Constitution and the Rules

The rules of the Book Society could have their own book, and this part of the archive swells with activity. Members have added or amended specific clauses regarding membership, attendance and even smoking as each committee has taken up governance. When the Society was first established, a simple constitution was written out to contain rules and membership clauses, and as it grew and took on more members, there would naturally be tweaks. In March 1925, it was reported that there were 44 members of the Society. Thirty--seven were in London, five in the rest of the country and two by correspondence only. By 1939, there were 75 members. There are no records through the war years, but the next count in 1948 shows that there were 35 publishers, 17 booksellers, and three publisher/booksellers. In 1968 there were two literary editors, one reader/

indexer, three librarians, three printers, one literary agent, 46 publishers, 35 booksellers and 14 authors, showing how many more branches of the book trade were joining up. In 2010 the membership included one archivist, six authors, four librarians, 22 in professional services, 29 booksellers, nine journalists, 15 literary agents, one printer, three who were uncategorised, and 28 trade body representatives. It is a shame that not every committee recorded their membership numbers, but they show how the Society grew and attracted members from both traditional and new areas of the industry.

When the Society was new, a decision was made to have no upper membership limit, but instead, people would have to receive a guest invitation from a member before they were formally suggested to the committee, and the first names granted this were Basil Blackwell and Stanley Unwin.

Another rule, created in 1936, stipulated that any members who missed two meetings of the Society without good reason in the same financial year would lose their membership. (This rule created much archive material, as the secretaries over the decades wrote to offenders, threatening to remove them.) In 1984, the constitution was amended to read that if three dinners were missed by a London member, or more than one by a member outside of London, then they would be ejected. As a result, many more letters were written to members in the 1980s and 90s, explaining to them that they would have to leave if they did not attend the next dinner. Sally Whitaker was possibly the strictest secretary on the matter of attendance, and it did not matter how senior the offender was. In 1981 she wrote to the prestigious non-fiction publisher Paul Hamlyn to tell him he was no longer welcome!

Although there were many committee meetings over the decades which discussed membership as a main topic, the story of how women were granted access to the Society as members is one that runs almost parallel. When the Society was founded, the all-male first committee wrote a clause into the constitution to disallow women from becoming members, but in 1927 Sidney Dark and David Roy (of WH Smith) proposed it should be deleted. A new clause was created which read:

Male guests may be brought by Members attending ordinary dinner-meetings of the Society, provided that any relevant regulations decided upon by the Executive Committee from time to time are duly observed; but the same guest shall not attend more than three such dinner-meetings in any calendar year.

As will be explored when we are at dinner, there were special event ladies' guest nights over the years, but as these were not considered what were termed as 'ordinary' meetings in the clause above, women could not be recommended for membership if they attended these evenings. The fact that women were not able to become members was a cause for debate at committee meetings over the decades, especially as they were employed in all sectors and at all levels of responsibility in the book trade. Ian Norrie's obituary carries the statement that he engineered the Society to accept bookwomen too[8], and he was indeed one of those on the committee who wanted to bring about this change. A vote was held in 1967, which saw 56 for allowing women entry into the Society and 46 against but it was decided that the numbers made it too close to call. It wasn't until April 1972, when the results of a ballot saw 65 for and 23 against that the resolution was finally passed that women could join the Society and the word 'male' was removed from clause 19. In November 1972, the committee welcomed the first seven women guests to dinner.

Another concern that continued to arise at committee meetings through the decades was the ageing and perceived narrowness of the membership. In 1973 a resolution was passed to bring down the age of members, and in August 1985, at a meeting held about the Society's purpose, it was agreed that the younger generation needed to be encouraged to join. On 7 March 1991, Ian Norrie, who was quite a vocal member of the Society, wrote to the committee to say that he felt they still needed to attract new members. The committee decided that they would start to give preference to younger candidates, and the secretary would write to retired members to ask them to stand down from overcrowded dinners. By March 1996, the retired members' category was dropped from the Society's constitutions, and there were to be no more honorary members of the Society. The committee also made amendments to the length of time the Deputy President or Chair could be

---

8. *The Times*, 6 October 2009, p. 57.

allowed to sit, from four years to one, but for the role of President it was left open-ended.

However, writing these rule changes into a heavily edited constitution would not solve all of the Society's issues. By the year 2000, Clive Bradley, then Chairman and the Chief Executive of the Publishers Association, took another look at the constitution, and at a sub-committee meeting, the point was raised that the Society should reflect a wider section of the population. In 2001 discussions continued and Chair Colin Whurr was noted in the meeting minutes as suggesting that it was time to 'see past the ageing white male' and make the Society more diverse. When publisher Francis Bennett took over the position of chair in July 2004, he brought forward these considerations about creating a community feel in the Society and began to push back against some past rigidities which were stifling the ability to grow the membership. He has provided a short piece which describes the work that he and his committee undertook in order for this to become a reality:

For years I only went to the Society's dinners as the guest of two great friends, Brian Bennett and Tim Rix. On the occasions my name went forward for election it was always rejected, perhaps because I did not get on with the Society's 'management' in the 80s and 90s! Imagine my surprise, pleasure and then anxiety when in a matter of weeks early in 2004 I was asked to join, become a committee member and then be the next Chair of the Society. I was given a simple instruction: 'Fix it or finish it'. Why? Because attendance had fallen to increasingly unsustainable numbers. So, with the

help, support and encouragement of a wonderful committee, we increased the numbers of members, and we invited
speakers who had real pulling power, making the Society a
place to which members of the book trade wanted to come.
It worked. It is one of the great pleasures of my career that
I had a hand in making the Society what it unquestionably
is today: a hugely successful and important part of book
trade life.

This achievement is on a par with the committee
decision in the 1970s to allow women as members of
the Society. Although the admission of women into the
Society was a huge and much-welcomed development
in its history, it is the committee vote on the name
change which will be more vividly remembered by
many members today. In the archive is a printed-out
Word document from 13 April 2011, written by the
secretary and Managing Editor of the Folio Society,
Sue Whitley, entitled 'CHANGING THE NAME'.
Underneath this heading, she described the original
name of the Society of Bookmen as sounding 'tweedy'.
However, some of the initial replacement names did
not meet her standards, and she described another, the
Society of Bookmen and Women, as 'too clunky' and
concluded that the committee would need to ask members to choose to keep the original name or change it
to her favourite, the Book Society. However, a couple
of months later, in June 2011, a decision still had not
been reached. In an email to committee members, a list
of name suggestions was shared, including the Book-
folk, the Society of Book People, House of Books and

the Book Worms. There was continuous discussion at committee meetings where 'The Name Change' became a regular agenda item. Interestingly, one of the first-ever women members thought it should stay the same, and she wrote to Sue to say that she believed the Society of Bookmen should be retained. Her rationale was that the Book Society was the name of the defunct book club mentioned earlier, which Walpole had also been involved in. However, Sue and the team behind the change got their way. The *Bookseller* reported on 5 December 2014 that the name of the Society of Bookmen had officially changed to the Book Society, but that the committee knew it had happened 'disgracefully late'. Those who pushed through this name change may not have realised it at the time, but they performed a major service to the Society by ensuring that its title would remain inclusive of all genders and identities in future decades. Amanda Ridout, who is a long-standing member, provided this important statement about her role in the name change:

As soon as I took up the role of Chair at the Society, everyone was asking me if I would get the name changed. It had seemed to me and to many others that a key strategy for broadening the membership and modernising the Society was to effect a change. There was much anecdotal evidence that younger female members of the industry were deterred from coming to dinners as well as considering membership because of the perception that the Society was outdated and non-inclusive. The committee had a short debate about a possible new name as we felt that time was of the essence and the previous delay had been excused by the inability to find a consensus around what that name should be. We settled on the Book Society quickly and then put it to an Extraordinary General Meeting in December 2014. The change was passed by a majority and the decision was almost universally applauded. One of the most endearing emails I received after the vote was from Philip Joseph – an elderly male member in his eighties – praising our courage and the outcome. We have never looked back since that decision and our ambition to attract a wider and younger membership as a result continues apace.[9]

There was another more technical and evolutionary reason that the Society's committee wanted to push through the name change, and that was so they could refresh their online presence. As the Society continued to modernise, the committees in place at the beginning of the 2010s, where the archive ends, created one last flurry of paperwork concerning the website's construction. Ideas were put forward around how members would be able to book their dinner slots, how the menus would be viewed when new people joined, and whether each person would need a user account and password. Inevitably the new website would ultimately lead to the end of the archive, which has been used to research this book. Not all of us remember a time before emails and word-processing software made the world of work more streamlined, or so we like to think, but the one area of the Society's activity that could not be trans-

---

9. Supplied by Amanda Ridout to the author over email, September 2022.

ported to the ether is the dinner, despite the might of the Covid-19 pandemic.

Now that you have been given a glimpse of some of the goings-on of the committee over the decades, it is finally time to gather up the papers, leave the meeting room and go to the main event. The very purpose of the Book Society, when it began under Walpole, was to encourage conversation between book trade professionals. So then, why not find your name card, place it where you want to sit, and, more importantly – not to rush you – but have you checked whether your guest has arrived yet?

4

Dinners, Guests and Speakers

If you cast your mind back to the Book Society's beginnings, you will recall that Walpole's intention for his dinners was for those in the British book trade to discuss important industry issues, whether they were an author, publisher, bookseller or librarian. As the membership numbers grew, these dinners began to be held in larger venues with invited guests in attendance, and from the mid-1920s, the introduction of a speaker transformed proceedings into the dinner events that we would recognise today. The heartbeat of the Society can still be heard amongst the clattering of knives and forks, the passing of the cheese and biscuits and the opening of bottles of wine around the tables filled with members and guests alike. So do pick your seat, and we shall begin the evening.

You may expect to look around and see the grandeur of the Savile Club, but that venue was not always where the Society gathered after its beginnings in Walpole's drawing room. When the first committee started to search for a suitable place to hold their regular meetings, their first idea was Stationers' Hall. Located in the City of London, right next to St Paul's Cathedral, the Hall is one of the few surviving elements of a publishing and bookselling district levelled in a Blitz raid which took place just after Christmas 1941. Dating back to 1403, the Hall had witnessed the development of the law of copyright and had been the first meeting place of the Publishers Association, founded in 1896, and the Booksellers Association, which came into existence a year before that. However, the Society could not afford a dinner there, even without wine, which had been suggested at one meeting in 1922 as a way to cut the cost. Although the committee decided to look elsewhere, then, there were a couple of special events held at the Hall to commemorate certain individuals or milestones.

Other venues were employed to house the Society dinners between the 1930s and the 1970s, and they included the Howard de Walden Club, the Old Colony Club, the Comedy Club and Kettner's restaurant. Some of these dining halls and clubs were frequented month after month, whereas others were chosen by the Chair or President at the time and then relinquished when new committees took over. Of them all, Kettner's was the most visited dining hall by the Society until the late 1970s, when their wine prices went up. It was then that the committee sought the price list of the Savile Club, and, it being much more agreeable, the Savile was first booked on 5 January 1978. It was recorded in meeting minutes that the committee had considered other places, including the Oxford and Cambridge Club and the Athenaeum, but noted that the Savile could provide its ballroom for £90 plus £6.33 a head, including a three-course meal and drinks. Since that first dinner there, the Society did not deviate away from the Savile until 2021, when a vote was called by then Chair Michael Bhaskar after the question of whether the Society should move was raised at an AGM. The result was in the affirmative, and so far, in 2022, dinners have been held at new venue The Conduit, which is situated in Covent Garden.

It may be remembered too, from the previous section, about the committee and its historic decisions that women were not able to become members of the Society until 1972. Until that date, they were instead invited to what were termed 'Ladies Nights'. The first such night was 2 May 1935 at the First Avenue Restaurant in central London, where the speakers were Dorothy L. Sayers and Eileen Power, and each guest received a complimentary National Book Token worth 7/6. The price of dinner was 5/-, and morning dress was requested. It was stated on the invite that 'Each member entitled to bring one lady guest. No men guests but members welcome to come alone.' There were those in the Society that wanted women to be able to come to the ordinary meetings as guests, too, and in 1948, Sydney Goldsack of Collins Publishers asked that it be taken to a vote. A ballot followed where 33 members said yes, 27 no, 16 abstained, and two said they were neutral. However, the committee decided not to proceed as they felt that these results were too close to call. By the 1960s, as the date got closer for women to be able to join the Society as members, they started to be invited to speak at male-only dinners.

The first of these was Marghanita Laski, who came to talk about her work as a reader for the Oxford English Dictionaries. There was more progress in May 1967 when the committee agreed that women guests were allowed at meetings as long as there was a woman speaker. The first time this occurred was on 1 June 1967, when novelist and literary critic Pamela Hansford Johnson took to the podium. When women could finally join men as members of the Society in 1974, this rule, now redundant, was dropped.

One guest at the Society dinners that became most unwelcome in the 1980s was tobacco. In this period, people could still smoke in various indoor places, including restaurants and bars, and there was advertising for cigarettes on television, on the sides of buses and at sports events. However, the committee of the Society at the time started receiving complaints from members, and therefore decided to send a questionnaire to all members to ask whether they would be against the introduction of non-smoking tables. Some responders were keen to point out that they smoked a pipe. Bookseller Nicholas Heffer asked, 'What is the world coming to?' on his returned slip, whereas literary agent Carole Blake wrote across her form, 'This is a very good idea', and publisher Ian Chapman said he would prefer not to sit next to a cigar smoker but 'I am not psychotic about it'. Publisher David Gadsby made clear that his preferred solution was no smoking at all, but another respondent raised a concern about forcing guests who were on the top table not to smoke. Smoking and non-smoking tables were implemented shortly after this ballot was collected, and the topic did not come up again.

With all these changes in mind, sitting at the table getting ready for a Society dinner would have been vastly different in the 1980s, with women present and smokers grouped together on separate tables than, say, in the 1920s, at a men-only gathering in Walpole's drawing room. Today there is a new venue and an acceptance that all who work in the British book industry can be members and guests. However, although the dinners have evolved as the decades have gone on, one element has stayed the same for nearly the whole duration of the Society's existence, and that is the famed speaker slot.

5

The
Speakers

At Book Society dinners held in the present day, after the plates are cleared away and coffee is served, the guest speaker will get ready to take their place at the front of the room. Most recently the podium has hosted David Shelley, CEO of the Hachette Group in London, and Society President Richard Charkin at the summer party in July 2022, the first in three years due to the Covid-19 pandemic. The years 2020–22 saw the biggest hiatus of dinners in the history of the Society, and now more than ever they are important events, not just socially but professionally, for members and guests alike. Depending on the events of previous decades, the speakers chosen by the committee have generally reflected the issues, challenges and innovations the British book trade has faced. Some have used their slot to impart to members and guests alike their wit and wisdom on a variety of subjects, ranging from the tribulations and the occasional good points of being an author, working extremely hard as a literary agent, managing large corporations or running small outfits. After the speaker is finished, they take questions from the floor, and all of this activity occurs under the Chatham House Rule, which is a universal term meaning that the contents of the speeches must not be shared outside the room.

This creates a valuable sense of freedom which allows members and guests alike to talk. The Society's archive reflects this rule from the word go, which means that although it contains the invitations and requests that were sent to speakers, there is no recorded narration of any of the speeches. You may therefore be forgiven for wondering what there is to write about here, but even though what was said may have been lost to the mists of time (unless, of course, you were there), what has been left for the rest of us allows for a fascinating exploration of the topics that were covered, revealing some of the big challenges and conversation points that have occurred in the British book trade during each decade of the Society's existence. In order to provide that picture, we will explore a selection of speeches through the decades. Let us start at the beginning, in the 1920s, when Walpole was still in the chair. Now please sit back and take a sip of your coffee.

On the first few occasions that the Book Society met, there were no dinners put on for guests, and the only people in attendance were the committee members. Then, on 14 February 1922, Walpole chaired a meeting where he asked for talks to be curated on a number of book trade subjects, and the following were thought up by members: bookseller Robert Bowes suggested one called 'The Art of Bookselling', whereas Stanley Unwin wanted to host one on book distribution abroad. John Irvine came up with the topic of 'Plays as Books' and Edmund Gosse wanted to focus on 'Publicity and the Book'. Sidney Dark suggested a lecture entitled 'The New Reading Public' and Hugh Dent wanted to focus the audience on the merits of colour printing. These initial ideas became a series of Society lectures which were available to all, costing 1/- to the public and 6d per head to the trade. Some of them were also written up into the circulars we looked at earlier in the section on the committee, and were meant to be instructional rather than inviting debate and conversation.

As explained in the first section, the speakers at these inaugural dinner parties delivered a series of lectures that continued through to the 1950s. Some other topics not already mentioned that were signed off by committees during this era include 'Books at Sea', which was about selling to libraries on cruise ships, 'What People Read and Why', 'Problems of a Literary Editor', 'Books and the BBC', and then the more dystopian topic 'Who and Where is the Reading Public?' Author J. B. Priestley did a talk in 1955 called 'Can Books Survive?' and in 1956, John Boon asked the audience at Kettner's, 'Is There a Future for Fiction?' These headings indicate that the British book trade was trying to solidify its identity and value to the consumer in the days before market research became easier, and these talks were about broadening the outreach of books to the public. By the 1970s, some publishing names we may still recognise – or indeed have been acquainted with – had their turn to speak about a range of trade issues or offer their insight. For example, Paul Hamlyn took to the podium in 1972 to impart his experience to a packed room, and in the same year, Charles Hammick, founder of Hammicks book chain, gave a talk on successful bookselling. Publisher John Murray gave the audience tales of his experience in 1979, and Oxford University Press celebrated five centuries of publishing at a special Society dinner in April 1978.

Several serious trade-wide issues have graced the dining room through the decades, ready for debate. In 1973, there was a dinner meeting to discuss the effect that the imposition of VAT on books would cause, and in 1979 an evening was held to discuss the victory of Public Lending Right (PLR) for libraries and whether it was a good regulation in terms of the business of publishing. The same year also saw a dinner about the National Book League, to remind publishers again what services they offered because there had been a lull in activity.

The 1980s saw considerable changes to bookselling, as companies opened several bookshops under the same brand or chain and applied new ways of serving customers and stockholding. Ainslie Thin, owner of Thin's bookshops, gave a talk in 1985 entitled 'Bookselling in a Time of Accelerated Change'. A year later, John Cooper, who worked for the Pentos group that had bought out Dillon's academic bookshops, spoke about why they had invested in the business and their infamous advertising campaign of the day. The words 'Foyled again? Try Dillon's' had been positioned on a bus shelter advertisement right outside Foyle's on Charing Cross Road, and caused a bit of a ruckus. Christina Foyle, who ran the business at the time, did not keep a neat shop, and she was known for it. Those who were around at this time will recall that the 1980s also saw the Net Book Agreement (NBA) start to be questioned by publishers and booksellers, including Cooper's boss, Terry Maher, who was in charge of the Pentos Group. The merits and pitfalls of not allowing books to be discounted was a topic that affected the whole industry. On 2 June 1988, the Society invited Michael Zifcak, chair of 38 book-shops in Australia, to explain how things were going after they'd abandoned price fixing in 1972. Meanwhile, a new bookseller on the block, Tim Waterstone, who had opened the first London branch of his now well-known chain in 1982, spoke twice this same year about how he was changing the face of book retail.

Although there was a lot to talk about in the world of bookselling, other topics were discussed in the 1980s. In 1985, Paula Kahn of the Longman Group spoke about women working in publishing and called her talk 'Is It Inevitable, and Shall You Enjoy It?' She pointed out that 60% of the publishing workforce at the time was made up of women, but that men still held many of the senior roles, showing how unequal the industry was and bringing it to the forum of the Society for discussion.

As publishing houses began to merge to create big-ger companies, there were talks from those heading up these developments. In 1989, Richard Charkin, then head of the Octopus publishing group, spoke about 'Changing Marketplaces', and the same year, histori-an and publisher Eric de Bellaigue was invited to speak about the 'Urge to Merge', in which he described how with Collins just sold, Hodder and Macmillan were the only two larger independent publishers left. One of the effects of all these mergers was that sales reps were abandoned in favour of in-house sales and marketing teams. Penguin Marketing Director Patrick Wright highlighted this move in his talk 'Death of a Salesman' in 1989, where he spoke about how the role of the rep had evolved and moved away from traditional selling to UK bookshops to retailers in other countries, thus expanding the export market in English language books. Along with changes to the old, there were new publishing houses being established that used the Society's dinners to share their new start-up initiatives, and one of the most notable in this category was Bloomsbury. In 1987, founder Nigel Newton spoke about how they were about to turn one year-old, and his talk was entitled 'Publishing: How Other People Do It'.

As the 1990s continued, the speakers at the Society dinners continued to discuss an ever-evolving book trade. In 1994, the Chief Executive of Penguin, Peter Mayer, spoke about how publishers needed to keep being significant in a time when many companies were becoming far more corporate and make sure that they still catered for the independent bookshop. In December 1990, after Christmas dinner had been eaten, Deputy Editor of the *Bookseller* Penny Mountain spoke about the role and relevance of book trade magazines. Liz Attenborough tackled the subject of commercial changes to publishing for children earlier that same year, using her experience as Publishing Director at Puffin, and Carole Blake spoke about the power struggles being felt between author, agent and publisher. In 1991, Sir Simon Hornby, chair of WHSmith, spoke about 'Book Retailing and the Future', and 1996 saw the company MD Alan Giles enlighten the dining hall on the possibly contentious topic of 'Getting Along with Publishers'.

In 1998, Tim Waterstone came back to the podium to let the dinner guests of the Society know that he believed his chain had won the fight between the larger book retailers. He termed his talk the 'Battle of the Booksellers', but there was one area that publishers and booksellers revered and feared equally, and that was new technology. For bookshops like Waterstones, new e-commerce systems, the introduction of barcodes and stock control mechanisms meant that they could, and did, grow. Back in 1995, Peter Kindersley educated the audience about the 'Coming of the Virtual Book', and tagged on a peek at the latest products Dorling Kindersley were working on to tap into the home computer market. But although there was opportunity, there was still fear of digital innovation, and Trevor Dickinson, an HMI for libraries, used his speaker slot in 1997 to ask whether there would be any readers left in the year 2000. In 2008 Bill Samuel, who was director of Foyle's, and Michael Holdsworth, formerly of Cambridge University Press, went further and held a heavily attended debate about whether bookshops would even exist on the British high street in five years. Two years later, the merits of Amazon as a customer or a competitor were being discussed by one of its retired MDs, Brian McBride, whilst another dinner speech given by

Santiago de la Mora from Google Books focused on how the internet was revolutionising choice and customer reach. In the same year, Stephen Page, CEO of Faber, addressed a need for publishers to behave differently to survive in a world where they were not the only creators of written content. Another related topic that came up at a few dinners over the decades was the effect of broadcasting on the industry, and the question of which areas they could collaborate on. In 1986, the Chief Executive of Channel 4, Jeremy Isaacs, spoke on the topic of television and the written word; similarly, Melvyn Bragg, in 1993, wanted help with his homework, and asked those present which books they thought would make good screen adaptations.

6

A
Note
on
Authors

Authors have spoken at Society events too, but unfortunately, the archive does not give much away about their
talks, apart from that they would be speaking about their
books and careers. Over the decades, there have been
notable bestselling and household names such as Melvyn
Bragg, Max Hastings, Julian Fellowes, Val McDermid,
Ben Macintyre, Michael Palin, Maeve Binchy, P. D. James,
Claire Tomalin, John Lloyd and John Mitchinson of *QI*
fame, and Kate Mosse. More recent speakers have included the likes of Chris Riddell, Adam Kay and Carole
Tonkinson.[10] However, a couple of talks left a bit more
evidence because, on occasion, depending on what was
happening around them, authors have brought their

---

10. NB A list of speakers at Book Society dinners from 2012–22 can
be accessed on the website.

concerns about the industry to the Society to seek opinion. In 1992, Deborah Moggach discussed being a novelist in a climate of change and how she established her career in what she termed challenging times for writers. In 1999, Maureen Duffy spoke about copyright regulations, which at the time were undergoing a series of amendments that Duffy saw as harmful to authors like herself.

7

Special
Events

As well as the dinner and speaker format that we and countless members and guests have become accustomed to, every summer, and then again around Christmas, the Society has put on special parties where the President says a few words to round off the year or celebrate the holiday season being upon us, and sitting down is replaced by standing up with a drink and a canapé or two. In terms of other notable dinner occasions, several have been held throughout the last one hundred years, to mark milestones or to remember the dearly departed. In 1961, the Society turned 40 years old, and President Sir Stanley Unwin highlighted its past achievements, in which he included one of his. Unwin imparted that in 1926 he encouraged the committee to visit the book trades in Amsterdam and Leipzig, a move that he admitted the Publishers Association were less than impressed with, but that he believed had since provided a lot of good practices for the industry. Unwin went on to reflect that when he made his speech, he was speaking as the only survivor of the first Society meetings held at Walpole's house. By 1971, when the Society held a members' only 50th anniversary dinner at Stationers' Hall, that link had disappeared entirely. Speakers included the then Chair, bookseller Ian Norrie, and President Ian Parsons, alongside some of the ex-chairs: Philip Unwin, Sir Basil Blackwell and Sir Robert Lusty. The accompanying dinner was asparagus soup, river trout *amandine*, saddle of lamb and orange syllabub.

In 1981 there was another dinner at Stationers' Hall to commemorate 60 years of the Society, and as Parsons had recently died, it was decided the dinner would be held in his honour. The menu was avocado mousse, fillet of sole *bonne femme*, and roast beef, then cheese, or caramelised oranges for dessert, with After Eight mints. The *Bookseller* marked the occasion in a special report, stating that a 'Golden Jubilee' had taken place and reminding readers of the Society's achievements, which included setting up the National Book League, and how Harold Raymond's idea of a National Book Token scheme was voted a good idea at a dinner. The committee requested two wine glasses per person for a special champagne toast to commemorate the life of publisher Charles Pick, who had worked at the top of several of the large houses, including Heinemann, where he reigned for 23 years. In 1982 the Society held a more reflective members-only meeting, entitled 'Candace or Criticus', where attendees were invited to the usual dinner and a more serious discussion over the relevance of the constitution, and debated such things as whether they were holding enough dinners each year and if more speakers were needed.

In December 1997, the Society's 75th anniversary dinner invite was headed 'The Sober Wisdom of Hindsight', and was again for members only. The menu this time was smoked salmon pate, noisettes of lamb, almond and pear tart with cream, and then coffee and champagne. A commemorative toast to publisher John Boon, who had recently retired as President after fifteen years, was made after coffee. Archival evidence points to an exceptionally good evening as a letter was sent out afterwards to all those who attended, politely mentioning that they needed to make a financial contribution to cover the sheer amount that was drunk. It also said, however, that 'if you were sober, then please be excused!' It turned out from a glance at the accounts for that year that the Society was £600 out of pocket, and in the end, all attendees were charged £10 each.

Amongst the dinner speaker events and the commemoration dinners were some evenings that were put on purely for fun. In 1960, a mock trial was held at Kettner's restaurant at which 'Ian Norrie will be charged with falsely claiming to be a bookseller pure and simple'. Basil Blackwell was a judge. In July 1991, a lavish Bookmakers' Ball was held at the Quayside restaurant in the World Trade Centre in London, and the evening was described on the invitation as an 'elegant buffet supper – Black Tie'. There were also years of Christmas quizzes, and in 1993, the invite stated that Father Christmas would be in attendance, distributing 'appropriate Christmas gifts'. More recently, Mark

Billingham's Criminally Complex Christmas Charity Quiz was advertised to members in November 2012, to raise money for the Book Trade Charity.

This is a snapshot of some dinners through the ages of the Book Society, and the speakers that provided debate and entertainment. Although we cannot talk much about what was said unless we were there, we can see the topics and discussions brought to the dining hall that were deemed important enough by the committee through the decades. The venue also may have changed over the years, but the structure of the evenings has remained remarkably close to that of the first dinner and lecture in 1924. So be sure to join in giving all the speakers a hearty round of applause. Once questions are over, it will be time to converse again before members and guests leave to catch the train, get into a cab, or even go on to somewhere nearby. This informal extra element of the evening should not be forgotten, for it is where connections can be made, and friendships developed. Therefore the third part of this history has been written with the help of Society members and guests, past and present, who you may just bump into when you go to get your coat. Whether you pass by at their tables for another glass, or end up in the cloakroom queue together, it is never easy to leave a Society dinner without being stopped at least once before you get to the door, so let us not make this night an exception.

8

The
Afterparty

After the speaker has received a hearty round of applause and questions have been asked by guests and
members alike, we have come to the end of the evening.
Well, kind of, because many members and guests will
now turn to their colleagues and counterparts for a good
old chat before they get sent on their way. Although I'm
sure you have found the archives of the Society fascinating, I, unfortunately, do not possess the power to
bring members and committees of the past back to write
something for this history, and it's quite difficult to use
the archive to do more than inform us of what happened
in the past. Even though I can tell you who actioned
what and who spoke at the dinners over the decades,
I cannot replicate the chatter, friendship ties, humour
and opinions of living, breathing members. However, I
did manage to track a few down, past and present, who
have no doubt stayed back at the end of many a Society dinner for an extra glass of wine and conversation.
They were asked a series of questions over email, and

the intention is that this part of the book will contin-ue the archive of the Book Society, their thoughts and comments preserved here to be accessed in future years. Within their reminiscences are yet more references to speakers and committee decisions made by some of them, or by others they knew, and some wishes for how the Society will evolve in the future. Some members responded with a neat paragraph for each answer, some spoke to me over the phone, and others wanted more space and sent whole essays, so let us try and listen to as many of them as possible before the time comes to leave the dining hall.[11] Their contributions are in no particu-lar order and in their own words (mostly). They will also introduce themselves and their careers to you, so make sure you keep an eye on the clock – you don't want to miss your train!

Richard Charkin

During my time as Chair, I think the Society improved the quality (or at least the popularity) of the speakers, the membership became younger and more diverse in gender terms, the finances were okay, we introduced a bit of technology, but we failed to address the issue of the name. I confess I was not too fussed either way but that was probably a reflection of my insensitivity. I was appointed President as far as I know as a simple ex-

---

11. NB Thank you to all who contributed to this part of the book; we could only accommodate a limited number of entrants.

pedient to prevent my resigning in a huff over what I thought was a breach of the governance rules when the name change (which I voted in favour of) was passed in dubious democratic terms. Being President has involved very little work but has engendered a real appreciation of the direction the Society has taken and its value in an ever-diverging book trade.

David Taylor

I think I was invited to join the Book Society committee around 2015, but I could well be wrong! I have an even vaguer recollection of my first dinner at what was then the Society of Bookmen, but I am pretty sure I was the guest of Toby Blackwell, and that must have been back in the early 1990s. However, I can be very specific about my time as Chair: from autumn 2017 to the summer of 2018. I managed to get a fairly eclectic range of speakers: Youngsuk Chi from Elsevier, in many ways – along with John Ingram – the midwife of print-on-demand; Justin Adams, then Managing Director of what was known as Connect Books (the artist formerly known as Bertrams); Bridget Shine, the fantastic CEO of the equally fantastic Independent Publishers Guild; and the Duracell bunny that is Jamie Byng of Canongate. Two publishers, a bookseller, and the leader of a trade body were a nice spread. I was also determined to get an author, and was delighted to secure Chris Riddell, the brilliant illustrator, who treated the attendees to a drawing masterclass during a unique evening. I had met

Chris many years before, in 1981, when he was going out with my future wife's middle sister, so a bit of a distant link! Chris and I might have been brothers-in-law if things had panned out a bit differently, but we had a good laugh about it, and he was a great speaker and an astonishing artist.

A hundred years for a society is quite a milestone, and the committee started thinking about how we might mark this occasion back in our meetings in 2016. Little did we know that Covid would intervene and mess up our plans a bit. Fairly quickly we thought of commissioning a short history of the Society, and I was very happy to be able to offer Ingram's services in the printing of this book. The Society has played a unique role in our trade: it is hard to think of a similar forum where booksellers, publishers, wholesalers, distributors, agents, printers and others can mingle together in a social setting. Many a deal has no doubt been hatched and many a partnership created over the dining tables and bars of the Society. Long may that continue, and here's to the next hundred years of conviviality!

Toby Faber

You can probably guess from my surname that my link with publishing comes through the firm founded by my grandfather, Geoffrey. He was a relatively early speaker at the Book Society in the 1930s, when to be invited to speak as the Chairman of a young firm was a big deal. There are certainly references in his diaries to it, and at least one reference in a letter to him being an amusing speaker, or words to that effect (I can't be certain that it's specifically about the Book Society, but I suspect it is). He may even have spoken more than once. By the end of his career, he was very much part of publishing's great and good.

Members of the Faber family have never really expected or been expected to enter the business, but when Matthew Evans (then Chairman and MD) asked me if I'd like to join as his assistant, with a view to taking over as MD, I thought I'd never forgive myself if I didn't give it a go. My career up to that point had taken me through investment banking and an MBA to three years at McKinsey as a management consultant. So I had good business experience and a love for publishing because of my family background, but little direct knowledge of it. I joined Faber in 1996 and became MD a year later, before leaving in 2001 to become a full-time writer (thereby completing, you might say, my journey from money to quality of life). These days I combine writing and lecturing with a continuing involvement in publishing; I am a non-executive director of Faber & Faber and Liverpool University Press, and Chairman of Faber's sister company Faber Music.

I think Jo Henry first proposed me as a member of the Society of Bookmen (as it then was). It was actually after I had left Faber, and she was on the committee at the time. I remember her description of the meeting where my name came up. There had been a discussion of the ideal attributes for new members, and Richard Charkin (then MD of Macmillan Publishers) had quoted the ideal person being an author with links to publishing. Jo responded, 'In that case, I've got the perfect person . . .' Richard had been surprised to learn that I was an author, which amused Jo because at the time I was writing a book for Pan Macmillan (I should probably say that Richard proved to be a very supportive publisher, and is now a good friend and a colleague on the Board of LUP). So I joined the society in (I would guess) 2003 and went onto the committee fairly soon afterwards. Francis Bennett had just become Chairman, and he clearly brought a lot of energy to the role. The Book Society is really flourishing now, and I think a lot of that can be traced back to Francis.

I enjoyed my year as Chairman from 2010 to 2011. I was able to call on a good variety of speakers, many of whom were popular. There's not really any rivalry between different Chairmen, but I think I was the first to have three 'sell-outs' in my year (Santiago de la Mora of Google Books, Stephen Page of Faber and David Young of Little, Brown). I failed dismally with any attempts at long-term reform, however. We all agreed that the name needed to change, but there were no good ideas for alternatives (at that time, the Book Society was still a book club). My one innovation was to not read out the names of guests during the dinner – I always felt it made people uncomfortable – but Jonathan Lloyd, my excellent successor, immediately reinstated it. These days I'm a less regular attender than I once was, but I still enjoy coming when I do. The main purpose, of course, is to meet people, and you could declare that the next speaker would be the new MD of Waterstones (unusually for the time, there wasn't one in my year as Chair) and get a guaranteed sell-out as a result. Then it would be announced at the last moment that they couldn't come and there would be no speaker – people would still be happy because the room was full (I'm sort of joking, but only partly).

Nicholas Clee

I must admit that I enjoyed the society even when it was at its fustiest – though I always found the Society of Bookmen name embarrassing. The convivial atmosphere reflected members' long acquaintanceships; on the whole, they liked each other. But it is a much more vibrant organisation nowadays. The membership reflects the industry, and the speakers are influential figures whom one wants to hear.

Jo Henry

My first job in the book trade was working for the literary agent A. M. Heath. Mark Hamilton (whose son Bill now runs the agency) was my boss. I left to join Victor Gollancz (then being run by the indomitable Livia Gollancz), working initially in the editorial department and then (after a short stint when I left to do some travelling) in the sales department, eventually becoming Sales Director in the late 80s. Fairly shortly after that, the company was sold to Houghton Mifflin and then, in turn, to Cassell – which is now, of course, part of the Hachette empire, within which Gollancz is a specialist SF imprint. I left shortly after the Cassell sale, joining a group intending to buy out the Health Education Authority's publishing arm. After the fairly spectacular collapse of the venture (a book we were publishing called *The Sex Education Handbook* was the subject of questions in parliament and had to be pulled the day before publication), I was rescued by Tim Rix, who wanted someone to run the market research company he'd set up, Book Marketing Ltd (BML), while the co-founder, Clare Harrison, was on maternity leave. Clare never came back, and I ran BML through various incarnations (as an independent company, owned by *Publishing News*, owned by Bower, owned by Nielsen Book) until I left Nielsen in 2018, when I joined *Book-Brunch*, the online trade journal I'd helped set up some ten years previously.

It was Tim Rix who introduced me to the – then – Society of Bookmen. I remember being very overawed by the great and the good who were members – needless to say, nearly all fairly elderly men at that stage! I think I was probably part of an attempt to recruit a more diverse membership, with Francis Bennett at the forefront of that modernisation movement.

I joined the committee a few years later and eventually found myself as Chair – I seem to remember I was voted into that position at a committee meeting I wasn't able to attend. Always a danger! My first speaker was the Irish author and screenwriter Ronan Bennett (and luckily for me, also my brother-in-law). He is very softly spoken, and the amplification facilities provided by the Savile were just not good enough for the job, so the first thing I did was persuade the committee to invest in a decent microphone. My second innovation was to push back the start time of the dinners from 6 p.m. to 6.30 p.m., feeling that most people would welcome not having to rush away from the office before 5.30 p.m.

Along with many other chairs of the Society, I was able to field an incoming MD of Waterstones as a speaker, in this case, Gerry Johnson, along with the Austen specialist John Mullan. Two speakers I sadly didn't succeed in securing were David Lammy, then Minister of Culture at DCMS, and Neil MacGregor, then at the British Museum. But I was hugely grateful for the support that so many of the members gave me as Chair, particularly in suggesting and helping recruit speakers, with several of these dinners being sold out. The change of name that was ushered in when Richard Charkin was Chair was long overdue, and the broadening of the membership and more recent innovations such as quiz nights and drinks, in addition to the dinners, have also been very good for keeping the Society relevant for those working in the book industry today.

Andrew Hayward

I initially met Trevor Goul-Wheeker when we worked on the first World Book Day committee. Then one day, he emailed me and said my name had come up at a Book Society meeting, and they realised I was not a member.

Would I like to join? I immediately said yes, please. The chance to be in the same room as my peers and my betters talking about books was a wonderful thing. Plus, the calibre of the speakers usually means that you learn something new. I see the Book Society as a crucible for publishing knowledge and a catalyst for new ideas and thoughts. A chance conversation can lead to new outcomes.

For a number of years, I have helped (or maybe hindered) younger members of the publishing world, so whenever possible, I try and take younger publishing friends as a guest. Publishing, of all industries, is about networking. And there is so much to learn in publishing.

I left Constable & Robinson in 2009 because I had gone deaf. It was truly impossible to carry on doing what I had been doing. My friends in the industry rallied around me and gave me great encouragement at a time when I needed it most. A lot of those friends are in the Book Society, so I can testify to the caring side of our industry. Most important, though, is the fact that the Book Society is a forum where people who care about books and literacy, surely the most fundamental skill of any society, can come together and encourage one another not to just sell the books our publishing houses have produced, but to grow the market for our books. I look around the dining room at the Savile Club at one of our dinners and rejoice in the amount of talent. The Book Society has come a long way in the last one hundred years; the next one hundred will be even more exciting and innovative.

Bill Samuel

I got involved in the book trade late in life when my aunt Christina Foyle died, and I joined the board of Foyles, where I was Vice Chair for the first few years of the twenty-first century. I joined the board of Batch in 2006 and its parent, the Booksellers Association, in 2009. I left the board of Foyles when it was sold in 2018 but remain on the board of the BA and Chair of Batch. I was invited to speak at the Book Society dinner in October 2002 when the delightful Sue Butterworth was Chair. The title of my talk was 'First Impressions of the Book Trade', and it attracted a total audience of 32 – the smallest, I believe, for many years, suggesting that either the members were not particularly interested in the views of a newcomer or that, given the chaos into which Foyles had sunk under Christina, they were unlikely to learn anything of interest from her nephew. I accepted the offer of one year's complimentary membership, and I have been a member ever since, spending a number of years on the committee.

I enjoy the dinners enormously. I cannot think of another trade-based social club where people representing all aspects of a particular industry – suppliers, customers, intermediaries, journalists and others – socialise so comfortably together. It has been through the Book Society that a number of people who were my competitors or suppliers have become my friends, and I have missed very few dinners since joining.

Sue Whitley

I joined the Folio Society in 1973 as a correspondence secretary. I had trained as a teacher and had spent the previous three years in Spain but I couldn't get a job on my return, so this was meant to be a temporary post. As it turned out, I was there for thirty-five years, becoming Editorial Director in 1984. The Folio Society was founded in 1947 by Charles Ede, who wanted to restore standards of printing, illustration and binding that had been lost during the war. It operated as a book club, with members buying four books a year. At first, these tended to be classics and reprints of various kinds, but this gradually changed, and we added original works to our list.

It was the best job in the world as far as I was concerned, but it was a bit of an oddity and, therefore, sufficient unto itself. I felt very much on the fringes of the publishing world. I cannot for the life of me remember exactly when I joined the Society of Bookmen, but I do remember who got me into it and why: Tim Heald, journalist and author, who was one of the relatively few writer members – probably because they couldn't, unlike publishers, put dinners on expenses. I don't remember it being quite such a problem then, but certainly, if you were bringing guests (and it was a convivial place to entertain), then being able to charge it was pretty useful. As a result, quite a high proportion of members were publishers and literary agents, compared to booksellers and printers.

Tim thought that there were two problems with the Society at the time – one that it was getting too elderly, and the other that there weren't enough women members. The name told you all you needed to know. I was invited because I was a young woman, which, as I must have been about fifty by then, was pushing it. I have had a lovely time there ever since, and my one great sadness writing this is that Tim is not around to consult – he was a very witty and very genial friend, and he did me a huge favour. I cannot remember who was Chair when I joined, but I have a feeling that I became secretary when Jane Carr was in the post, and that it was during her tenure that the idea of changing the name was first canvassed. There was a lot of resistance, partly because of the rear-guard action of some of the older members, who wanted to protect its historic foundations as the brainchild of Hugh Walpole, but mostly because it seemed almost impossible to agree on an alternative: the Society of Book People (horrible), the Society of Bookmen and Bookwomen (too much of a mouthful) and practically anything else, too bland and not about the members. In the end, relatively recently, the Book Society was agreed on.

I resisted being lined up to be Chair because, as a director of a publishing company that specialised in dead authors, I didn't really know anyone. Thanks to Tim, the Society did ensure that I got out a bit more and actually met my fellows in the book trade. I have made wonderful friends over the years, of whom the most enduring is Francis. When Francis Bennett became chair, we were able at last to tackle the dwindling membership. We needed to get younger active members in, but felt that they would not spend their hard-earned spare time unless they too were meeting people who could be helpful and useful in the publishing sphere. I think the maximum number of members at the time (probably to do with what the Savile Club could accommodate) was 200, so we resolved the problem by making all those who were retired honorary members – no subscription to be paid, but they could come to dinners whenever they wanted to. That freed up room for new members, and a better balance was achieved. There were so many wonderful talks – the Chatham House rule always applied, so some speakers were quite outspoken, which was very entertaining. Too many good ones to choose, I think, but I do remember Quentin Blake (partly because I asked him, and he did it so well) and Clive Stafford-Smith, because he knew a prisoner on Death Row in America with whom I had been corresponding (and visiting) and it was so good to meet someone I admired so much.

Jane Carr

After graduating in 1971, I joined what became Cassell Macmillan as Publicity Assistant and then Publicity Manager. I joined Penguin in 1974 in the publicity department and moved to the export department in about 1976 to become Subsidiaries Liaison Officer. In 1980 I joined the British Library, then situated in the British Museum, as Marketing Manager for BL Publishing.

In 1999 I left the BL and moved away from the book world to become Executive Director of the Institute of Masters of Wine, but returned to books to become Chief Executive of ALCS, the Authors' Licensing and Collecting Society, in 2004. After semi- retirement in 2006 I continued to work for ALCS, to edit the *Journal of Wine Research* and to do some occasional freelance editing.

I seem to remember that I was invited to the Book Society dinners as a guest by Philip Joseph and Tim Rix, and possibly others, before I was approached (in the King's Library at the British Museum, as it happens) by Sally Whitaker, to ask if I would like to become a member. Like Groucho Marx, I did not, and do not, think of myself as particularly clubbable, if that is a word; but I found that I very much enjoyed the dinners. They were a way of keeping in touch with mainstream publishing, and of seeing old friends and making new ones. I also tried to invite people from the library as well as publishing worlds, and to create a bridge between the two. Although I enjoyed the talks, and found it easy to participate, the social and semi-professional side were probably more useful to, and enjoyable for me at that time. I do remember, at one of the early dinners when we had just moved to the painted-ceiling dining room in the Savile, walking into the members' dining room after our dinner to be greeted by a shout of 'Good God, a woman!'

I cannot remember when I came on to the committee, but I was selected as the first female Chairman – how ironic I found it to be the first female Chairman of the Society of Bookmen (I was followed by the wonderful Carole Blake). When the lovely John Boon was still President, he died during my term as Chair, and I led the search for the new Chair, Martyn Goff. I do remember that the task of finding ten good speakers a year was not an easy one; it could take time and sometimes considerable arm-twisting. I remember inviting Sandy Wilson to come and talk about the history and plans for the new British Library. He was at his most charming and intelligent, and I had several letters of appreciation following his speech – a rarity during my time.

Trevor Goul-Wheeker

After a marketing and senior executive career with the likes of Unilever and Gestetner, I entered the book trade in 1994 by sheer chance as MD of Hammicks Bookshops. After I had helped return the business to growth and profitability, Hammicks was sold to Ottakar's, now part of Waterstones, while the Hammicks Legal division was sold to John Smith & Son in 2003. I was elected to the council of the Booksellers Association in 1996, where I became a director and honorary treasurer, and was able to play a key role in the inception of World Book Day, becoming Chair in 2000. I was honoured with a Nibbie (British Book Award) for WBD in 2001, and a further Nibbie for Services to Bookselling followed in 2002. In 2003, I joined WHSmith as Executive Director to help develop a new books strategy, converting to a non-executive role on becoming CEO of Reed Health Group. I returned to the book trade in 2008 as Chairman of Haven Books Ltd, which supplies book collections to schools under the Pandora and Badger publishing brands. In 2009, I was invited to join Blackwell's as a non-executive director and was appointed Chairman in 2010. After ten years, during which Blackwell's growth and performance improved to the brink of profitability, I retired and was very touched to be honoured with the BAMG's Outstanding Contribution to Bookselling Award in 2019.

I was invited to speak at a Society of Bookmen dinner when Vice Chair of World Book Day in 1999, and I recall a room full of elderly men, most of whom were already asleep by the time I rose to give my talk ... and the rest had nodded off by the time I had finished. The invitation to join followed, and despite my qualms about what appeared to be an elitist, overwhelmingly male care home for the book trade, I decided to accept and work with others to broaden and diversify its membership and create a more relevant and vibrant Society.

I have been fortunate to be present for many candid, enlightening and extremely funny talks, but above all, the Book Society became the ideal meeting place for people from right across the book trade: authors, agents, publishers, printers, wholesalers, booksellers, and all those providing additional services to our industry. The Society has created a unique 'neutral' environment for all these people to raise ideas, discuss issues and sometimes even resolve contentious problems. I have already mentioned above the first time that I spoke and was invited to join the committee in 2011, where

I was delighted to help Amanda Ridout have the Society's name changed to the Book Society in 2015. On unexpectedly becoming Chair in 2015, I was surprised to find the Society losing money and facing a number of challenges related to unpaid or underpaid membership fees, falling membership/attendance and an outdated constitution. It was rewarding to see these matters addressed over the year that followed, the Society return to financial health, and the growing and increasingly diverse membership and attendance achieved by subsequent Chairs.

Jo Howard

Jo spoke over the phone about her career at WHSmith, as chair of World Book Day and now as a publishing coach and leadership development expert. As a female member of the Book Society, Jo first attended as a guest with WHSmith colleagues, then stood in for her boss before being elected in her own right by Sue Butterworth, who was Chair at the time. At one of her first dinners, Jo remembers hearing the announcement 'Do ladies mind if the gentlemen remove their jackets?' But aside from the lingering old-fashioned etiquette, she enjoyed the Society immensely because it made her feel part of something, and the evenings were filled with good conversation and fun. Jo remembers that one particular dinner speaker in the 1990s was the children's illustrator Anthony Browne, who drew a dot in the middle of a flipchart and invited the room to jump up and add to it. She remembers leaping up and running across the usually staid dining room at the Savile Club to join in! Jo is still a member of the Society today.

Charly Nobbs

In 1975 I joined a group of publishers – Chatto & Windus, Bodley Head, Jonathan Cape and Virago Press – when they opened a distribution operation which later became Grantham Book Services. In 1988 I moved to Cambridge University Press, responsible for customer service, inventory management and distribution. I joined Wiley in 2003 to head up distribution and customer services in the UK, Singapore and Australia, then in 2014 I was appointed Vice President, Global Supply Chain, responsible for the global distribution and inventory management of all Wiley book and journal products in print. In this role, I implemented, along with my teams, many supply chain improvements in a number of locations to ensure that we consistently provided a cost-effective and market-leading service to all our internal and external customers. I am now a freelance consultant, working globally to improve many areas of publishing and associated supply-chain processes. I really enjoy attending Society events, which showcase just how friendly and collegiate our industry is. One never knows how conversations during these occasions may develop, but they are always interesting and stimulating. Long may the Society continue!

Cathryn Summerhayes

I think I was first invited along as a guest to the Book Society dinners by Richard Charkin when I was working at Colman Getty on the Booker Prize, amongst others – and then as my career as an agent started to progress, I came along a number of times with the likes of David Shelley, Trevor Goul-Wheeker – and then my current colleagues Sheila Crowley, Jonathan Lloyd and Gordon Wise. I won the Nibbie for Agent of the Year in 2019 and was encouraged to become a member – and started bringing along my own friends from publishing, including Anna Valentine, Paul Baggaley and many more. I remember my author Adam Kay causing a stir for talking about audiobook pricing – you could hear the sighs and sucking in of air from many publishing folk – but he made us all laugh, too. I remember hearing Perminder Mann and her call to arms about the lack of diversity in the industry long before Black Lives Matter. I remember being at the naughty table at my last dinner before lockdown – in the same dress as Anna Valentine from Trapeze – and really feeling a part of such a friendly, welcoming bunch of similar people. I MISSED THOSE DINNERS – I MISSED THE PEOPLE.

I think that the Society remains a relevant body of people, and we should continue to answer the important questions about publishing that need answering more than ever in extraordinary days. Publishing is an industry that thrives on its people, its parties, its unexpected conversations at random events. We need to get through this time, and we will – if only because we all adore books and the people associated with them.

James Spackman

My first experience of a Book Society dinner was in 2006 as the guest of Roland Philipps, then my boss at John Murray. I had made the move to JM the previous year, having started my publishing career in the glamorous surroundings of the Bloomsbury Publishing post room, then escaped into roles in sales and marketing. It took a while for my astonishment at the Savile Club's camp aesthetic and the distinctly high-powered crowd to calm down and for me to realise Roland had done me a huge favour by seating me next to Ion Trewin. I spent the next hour or so hanging on his every word as he described the genesis of *Schindler's Ark*, a story that encapsulates so much about what a publisher is actually for in the world.

Some years after, now a member of the Society, I looked around the dining room as a speaker described the publishing industry's diversity problem to a quiet chorus of yups and hmms and thought, 'I wonder if there's a practical thing we can all do?' It struck me that virtually everyone there would have room in their house for a guest, and how helpful that could be to a publishing hopeful who did not (like I did) fit the classic mould of white middle-class southerner with parents they could stay with in London while they do their internship. That was the origin of the Spare Room Project, which, since 2016, has been helping people make a start in the industry by introducing them to friendly publishers with a spare room or – in lockdown – thirty minutes of time for an online chat (the Spare Zoom Project). My sincere hope is that the Society devotes its energy to opening up the industry to the people who deserve it: clever, committed book lovers of every background.

Alan Giles

I first attended an event of what was then the Society of Bookmen in the mid-1980s as the guest of Paul Scherer, the head of Transworld. I was the newly appointed head of the Books team at WHSmith. Paul was a wonderful host and would, in his inimitably charming manner, push back all attempts to refuse offers of lunch or dinner with 'but my dear boy, you have to eat'. Hence I attended my first Society dinner, and although it felt like I was much the youngest attendee, I received a very warm welcome despite the trade's reservations about WHSmith at the time. I was subsequently invited to become a member and was a reasonably regular attendee for much of the remainder of that decade, the 1990s and the first half of the 2000s. I was moved by WHSmith to a role at their ill-fated DIY subsidiary in 1988, but returned to the book trade as Managing Director of Waterstones in 1992. In 1998 I became CEO of HMV Group until I retired from executive life in

2006, becoming a member of the Book Tokens board until 2013.

In the 1990s, I was a committee member for a period and worked with Paul Scherer and others on a plan to modernise the Society and attract a younger, more diverse membership. Although well intentioned, the initiative was perhaps ahead of its time; the Society found it hard to shrug off its image of being a club for elderly white males (not helped, I think, by its use of the Savile Club, excellent as that is in many respects). At the time, a sceptic would view the Society as one of the ways in which the Whitaker family (owners of the *Bookseller* at the time) kept themselves closely informed about what was happening in the trade – David Whitaker was a central force in the Society, and for many years his sister Sally was the secretary. But it was always much more than that, a convivial 'safe space' where commercial rivalries could be set aside in a spirit of goodwill and bonhomie. I had the privilege of being the guest speaker on a couple of occasions, once when I was at WHSmith (talking to the Society is something of an initiation ritual for all who are appointed to run the books team at Swindon) and then when I ran Waterstones. In both roles, my employer was viewed with a mixture of admiration, suspicion and fear because of its commercial power, but as ever, the questioning was civilised, constructive and pertinent.

My favourite memories are inevitably about the colourful characters who were members, and I cherished getting to know participants from parts of the trade I would otherwise not have met. The Society is, I feel, a manifestation of what is unique about the book trade. In any other industry, such a society would either be a front for a cartel, or be highly political, or quickly outlive its usefulness. Those who work in the book industry do so not just because it is a vibrant commercial sector (true as that is) but also because of an absolute conviction that as instruments of ideas, books make a vital contribution to the cultural and educational welfare of a civilised society. The Society is the very embodiment of that ethos, and that is why it still flourishes a century on.

Suzanne Collier

I was first approached to join the Society of Bookmen (as it then was) in 1989. I was Chair of the Society of Young Publishers, and I received a phone call at my place of work, which was Andre Deutsch Ltd, in the days that Andre ran the company. It was like being invited into a special secret society, and I was truly honoured to receive such a call. However, in my other ear, I had repeated calls from Andre Deutsch to go and bandage his foot, which he had hurt skiing. This was long before the days of mobile phones, and I had to explain apologetically to the gentleman on the phone, who would not give me his name, that he would have to phone me back in thirty minutes as when Andre called, I had to respond immediately! Needless to say, he never phoned back, and it was not until a few years ago that the invitation to join was remade.

What I enjoy most about the Society is meeting many other publishers in a rather sociable environment. The speakers are always excellent, but sitting at the same table as other publishers, who you might not usually get to talk to, is always great fun. Plus, the parties! I always promise myself I will only drink one glass of fizz; yet, as if by magic, the one glass automatically refills.

Catherine Burke

In 2001 I was hired as an Editorial Assistant at BCA (Book Club Associates), where I sold books to the 1 million UK members of the World Books Book Club. After that, I joined Mills & Boon and helped launch and then ran the commercial fiction imprint MIRA. In 2010 I joined Little, Brown as Editorial Director of Sphere Fiction. I was promoted to Associate Publisher in 2012 and Fiction Publisher in 2013. I became Director of Hachette Audio UK in 2014, Executive Director of Group Rights in 2016 and was promoted to Deputy Managing Director of Little, Brown Book Group in 2019, now also overseeing Sphere non-fiction and the Little, Brown design team.

I believe my first invitation was from David Hicks, Chair of BTBS, where Arnaud Nourry was speaking, and David kindly thought of me as I was working at Hachette. I was invited to a few more dinners by colleagues at Hachette after that, and was invited to be a member by agent extraordinaire Sheila Crowley, who is on the current executive committee. I have really enjoyed the opportunity to network with others in the industry, and every dinner feels incredibly special. It has also been an opportunity to hear some very impressive, interesting and inspiring speakers, and I enjoy disagreeing with them almost as much as nodding along with what they say. Covid has made such a difference to membership this year, and it will be hard to evolve in post-Covid times. However, now we are all immersed in communicating via screen and across distances, opening up overseas membership could be worth considering, as well as arranging events such as charity quizzes. I feel I am just at the start of my membership, and I would love to contribute and play a role in keeping the Society a positive and lively one as it moves into its next one hundred years.

Gwyn Headley

In 2010, Jonathan Nowell of Nielsen Book Data invited me to a Society of Bookmen dinner at the Savile Club. I'd never been before, thinking it was perhaps a little stuffy for me, but I was astonished to find almost everyone I'd ever known gathered in one room. It was enormous fun, and the speaker (I can't remember who it was) was riveting. I couldn't believe I hadn't been before, so when Jonathan asked if I'd be interested in joining, I jumped at the chance.

I'm not a great one for committees, so I have never put myself forward for any office in the Book Society. I'm on the periphery of publishing anyway and don't have a mainstream publisher to represent, so I'm content to enjoy the food, the drink and the camaraderie. It's great to see old and meet new friends, and I have greatly missed the sociability during this year of lockdowns. The only contribution I've made outside simply enjoying the membership is to provide one speaker – Mike Shatzkin, the publishing guru and digital evangelist from New York. Mike and I have been good friends for over 40 years, and we settled into a routine; he would fly to London from NYC, hop into my car, and we'd drive to the Frankfurter Buchmesse. After the fair, we'd drive back to London, and he'd then fly back to New York. One year the Book Society dinner and Mike's trip to Frankfurt coincided, and I proposed him as a speaker. He was, as expected, fluent and controversial, and he predicted a dystopian future for publishing without bricks and mortar bookshops and the great majority of titles being sold as eBooks.

I see the Book Society as a society of friends with common interests, not as an austere business forum. For as long as people want to meet and talk together – and are allowed to – it will continue to thrive.

Suzanne Wilson-Higgins

I think I am the only member of the Book Society to have worked as an author, publisher, bookseller and printer (never been an agent, though)! I joined the book trade in 1990 at the age of 29 as a Commissioning Editor for business books at Heinemann, part of Reed

International plc based in Oxford. In each of the five following years, that group went through significant change, including a merger with the Dutch publisher Elsevier. I shuttled between Oxford and Michelin House for a couple of years, working on consumer and professional digital projects across all of Reed International Books. Following maternity leave, I moved to Blackwell's in Hythe Bridge Street and believe I became the first female board director of B. H. Blackwell Ltd in 1997, following a tempestuous board shake-up. My five years at Blackwell's were also a time of constant change, driven by the shareholders and a succession of management consultants, and ending in the selling-off of the cash cow division that historically sustained the group. In July 2000, I was recommended by Blackwell's to the Ingram family, who had set up Lightning Source Inc and wanted to establish a UK-based version of this print-on-demand and eBook service for UK publishers, initially to export their books to the USA and to supply eBooks to that emerging digital market. Lightning Source UK Ltd was launched at the Groucho club that year, and I was Commercial Director for the next decade, overseeing rapid growth. Following consulting stints with the Book Depository and an Indian publisher services company, in 2011 I joined Christian book publisher Lion Hudson as Sales Director and subsequently Managing Director, where I navigated the company's assets through more turbulent times and have especially enjoyed publishing children's books. I wrote a book on print-on-demand books for Elsevier in 2018. I expect to celebrate a decade at Lion Hudson in January 2021, and my 31st anniversary in book publishing in May 2021 . . . it has never been dull!

Michael Holdsworth of Cambridge University Press invited me to my first dinner, and I joined, having been proposed by the CEO of BTBS, David Hicks. The Christmas quizzes with John Mitchinson were great fun, and it was lovely to catch up with John Lloyd as our children were school friends. I love keeping in touch with old colleagues, Richard Charkin and David Taylor, among others. Retailers have been the most interesting speakers to me: Christopher North from Amazon.co.uk was an eye-opener; James Daunt gave an excellent talk when he first moved to Waterstones, which felt contro-versial at the time; and Trevor Goul-Wheeker provided an insightful update about my old employer Blackwell's. I think it is marvellous that the Society is celebrating its centenary, as it provides a unique forum for four key pillars of the book trade: agents, publishers, booksellers and printers.

Piers Russell-Cobb

I first worked in book publishing in 1971 in the pub-licity department of Jonathan Cape. Then in 1975–6, I was employed by the service company Chatto, Bodley Head and Cape. I returned from living in LA in 1977 to take a job at Marshall Editions, where I researched and wrote, with Quentin Crewe, chunks of *Great Chefs of France*. From 1978 to 1987, I worked for Thames & Hudson as International Marketing Manager, where

I launched and edited the 100k+ circulation free trade paper *Undercover*. I was headhunted in 1988 to go and work at the Reed Group – I started as co-editions person at Conran Octopus before being recruited to be Marketing Director (Publicity and Promotions) at Heinemann, which I left in 1991. I was Deputy Chairman of the Philip Wilson publishing group in the 90s. Through Media Fund (an M&A company I founded in 1991), I became an investor in Arcadia Books Limited, and about four years ago, I took over as publisher of Arcadia Books. When I worked at the Reed Group, Barley Allison (of Allison and Busby) invited me to be her guest at the Society of Bookmen dinner. From then, my attendance as a guest became more regular – I cannot remember how I was elected a member. The Book Society encourages enthusiasm for all aspects of the book trade, and is effective at inviting speakers in positions of influence, from CEOs to those who have an interesting take on the industry.

Emma Lowe

Being a part of The Book Society for me has always been a privilege. I fell into publishing by way of a maternity cover on a sales role at the London Book Fair and have never wanted to leave. Twelve years at the Fair helped me form the idea that publishing people care enormously about what they do and who they work with. Eight years at The Bookseller has cemented that belief. Being invited to be a part of The Book Society and ultimately becoming the secretary was an honour. I was very glad to be able to help preserve and promote the unique atmosphere of genuine care and interest in other humans that existed at every event.

Vivienne Wordley

I have held held positions at various publishers including Faber, Thorsons and Pan Macmillan before becoming Commercial Director at Foyles and founding Programme Director of the Emirates Airline Festival of Literature.

I don't recall the date I joined the Book Society, but I do remember that the early dinners I attended as a guest, where highly enjoyable, but distinctly male-dominated and rather traditional. When I became chair the committee spent time analysing the membership (just 66% of whom were active) and dinner attendees with a view to addressing the gender imbalance, building an audience for our speakers that was more representative of the current publishing industry and ensuring a networking society that was attractive to younger professionals.

We experimented with a diverse range of speakers including digital change leaders Mike Shatzkin (The Idea Logical Co) and Sophie Rochester (The Literary Platform); Rachel Russell (WH Smith, Books Director); Jude Kelly (Artistic Director, Southbank Centre and Founder of Women of the World Festival); Clive Stafford-Smith (human rights lawyer and founder of Reprieve). A Christmas Quiz, hosted by Mark Billingham helped raise funds for The Book Trade Charity and a new website enabled easier communication with the membership.

I think The Book Society will continue to evolve as a diverse meeting place that can cater for the twenty-first century – and an opportunity to meet in person.

Goodbye, until next time

It is time to leave the dining hall, and these views and anecdotes are what we managed to hear amongst the shuffling to get coats and the last drops of wine being poured. As you have read what these members said when they were asked whether the Book Society would continue to be the dining club for those in the book trade of the future, you will note their responses were a resounding yes. After the disruption of Covid-19 in 2020, which saw the whole industry having to deal with circumstances beyond their control, we now face more uncertainty with a cost-of-living crisis, war in Ukraine and a huge hike in energy bills. Paper and glue prices are also skyrocketing. These topics will no doubt become the subject of further talks that the Society hosts in their new venue, alongside those equally important considerations of being more diverse and opening the doors to all of us who work in the twenty-first-century British book industry. Additionally, the companionship, camaraderie and general antics at any given Society dinner and talk will no doubt continue. Walpole's original rationale behind creating his little dining club was to bring the industry together to talk and share ideas, and that concept is what should be continued for another hundred years. It is our hope that you have enjoyed this evening with the Book Society, and are looking forward to many more to come. See you at the next dinner.

9

List of Presidents and Chairs of the Book Society

Founded in 1921 by Hugh Walpole as the Society of Bookmen

Presidents

1921–1941	Hugh Walpole
1947–1968	Stanley Unwin
1969–1980	Ian Parsons
1981–1996	John Boon
1997–2013	Martyn Goff

2013–2022   Richard Charkin
2022–   Amanda Ridout

Chairs

1921–1922	W. B. Maxwell/ G. A. E. Marshall
1922–1931	Theodore Byard
1932–1936	G. B. Bowes
1936–1946	Gerard Hopkins
1946–1950	Basil Blackwell
1950–1953	Ian Parsons
1953–1956	Rupert Hart-Davis
1956–1959	James MacGibbon
1959–1962	Philip Unwin
1962–1965	Robert Lusty
1965–1968	Alan Hill
1968–1971	David Holloway
1971–1974	Ian Norrie
1974–1977	Gordon Graham
1977–1980	Colin Eccleshare
1980–1982	Brian Bennett
1982–1984	Martyn Goff
1984–1986	David Whitaker
1986–1988	Ion Trewin
1988–1990	Stephen Green
1990–1992	Tim Rix
1992–1994	Michael Turner
1994–1995	Ernest Hecht
1995–1996	Chuck Elliot

1996–1997	Jane Carr
1997–1998	Carole Blake
1998–2000	Clive Bradley
2000–2001	Colin Whurr
2001–2002	Philip Sturrock
2002–2003	Sue Butterworth
2003–2004	Alastair Niven
2004–2005	Francis Bennett
2005–2006	Jo Henry
2006–2007	Jessica Kingsley
2007–2008	Richard Charkin
2008–2009	Sonny Leong
2009–2010	Nicholas Clee
2010–2011	Toby Faber
2011–2012	Jonathan Lloyd
2012–2013	Vivienne Wordley
2013–2014	Simon Jude
2014–2015	Amanda Ridout
2015–2016	Trevor Goul-Wheeker
2016–2017	Rebecca Smart
2017–2018	David Taylor
2018–2019	Sheila Crowley
2019–2022	Michael Bhaskar
2022–2023	Jamie Hodder-Williams

Lightning Source UK Ltd.
Milton Keynes UK
UKHW041534301122
413126UK00001BA/1

9 781838 303686